MAY 2013

Ripley's Believe It or Not!

Developed and produced by Ripley Publishing Ltd

This edition published and distributed by:

Mason Crest
370 Reed Road, Broomall, Pennsylvania 19008
www.masoncrest.com

Printed and bound in the United States of America.

First printing
9 8 7 6 5 4 3 2 1

Ripley's Believe It or Not!
Curious Creatures
ISBN-13: 978-1-4222-2565-3 (hardcover)
ISBN-13: 978-1-4222-9240-2 (e-book)
Ripley's Believe It or Not!—Complete 16 Title Series
ISBN-13: 978-1-4222-2560-8

Library of Congress Cataloging-in-Publication Data

Curious creatures.
    p. cm. — (Ripley's believe it or not!)
ISBN 978-1-4222-2565-3 (hardcover) — ISBN 978-1-4222-2560-8 (series hardcover) — ISBN 978-1-4222-9240-2 (ebook)
1. Animals—Juvenile literature. 2. Curiosities and wonders—Juvenile literature.
QL49.P755 2012
590—dc23
                                2012020336

PUBLISHER'S NOTE
While every effort has been made to verify the accuracy of the entries in this book, the Publisher's cannot be held responsible for any errors contained in the work. They would be glad to receive any information from readers.

WARNING
Some of the stunts and activities in this book are undertaken by experts and should not be attempted by anyone without adequate training and supervision.

Ripley's Believe It or Not!®

Disbelief and Shock!

CURIOUS CREATURES

www.MasonCrest.com

CURIOUS CREATURES

Amazing animals. You won't find critters

more peculiar than this bunch! Read about

the incredible winged cat; the crazy half-zebra,

half-horse, or "Zorse;" and the beetle that is

longer than a human hand!

Odin the Bengal tiger takes a dip at the Six Flags Discovery Zoo in Vallejo, California.

CROCODILE ATTACK

Veterinarian Chang Po-yu lost his arm to the jaws of a saltwater crocodile in Shaoshan Zoo in Kaohsiung, Taiwan, on April 11, 2007.

The vet's forearm was bitten clean through when he reached through iron railings to remove a tranquilizer dart from the 440-lb (200-kg) reptile. Two bullets were immediately shot into the neck of the crocodile, which then dropped the arm. But this story has a doubly remarkable ending. First, the crocodile was unharmed by the gunshots as the bullets didn't penetrate its hide, they merely shocked the croc into opening its mouth; and second, a team of surgeons operated for seven hours to reattach the arm—successfully!

What was it like, Mr. Chang?

Reptilian Tales

CROC PLUNGE

Believe it or not, a crocodile suffered nothing worse than a broken tooth after falling from the 12th floor of an apartment block in the Russian city of Nizhny-Novgorod. It was the third time that the pet croc, named Khenar, had tried to escape his captivity by climbing through a window.

GREAT ESCAPE

Australian rancher David George spent a week clinging desperately to the branches of a tree to avoid being eaten by crocodiles. Stranded in crocodile country after falling off his horse and hitting his head, George climbed a tree and stayed there for six days and nights, terrified by the red eyes of the hungry crocodiles that were circling expectantly below. Surviving on just a packet of cheese-and-ham sandwiches and a few sips of water, he was eventually spotted by rescuers and hauled to safety.

DEADLY HEAD

A man in Prosser, Washington State, was hospitalized after being bitten by the decapitated head of a rattlesnake. Danny Anderson beheaded the 5-ft-long (1.5-m) rattler with a shovel, but when he reached down to pick up the severed head, it bit his finger, injecting venom. He took the head to a hospital, and by the time he arrived his tongue was swollen and the venom was spreading. He was released after two days' treatment. The bite was thought to be a reflex action from the snake, as, believe it or not, snake heads can still be dangerous up to an hour after being separated from the body.

HEARTY MEAL

U.S. scientists have discovered that some snakes can survive without food for up to two years by digesting their own hearts. Snake hearts then quickly rebuild themselves after a nutritious meal.

I am a veterinarian and a director of the zoo. When I anesthetized and treated the crocodile, the animal took my left-hand away suddenly. It was a huge shock in my mind, my limb felt pretty numb.

My left-arm caused extreme pain, but I told myself that I must live, I want to take my arm back, and do my best to connect it again.

My associate helped me to stop bleeding by pressing on the top of the arm until the ambulance came. When I was on the way to the hospital, the police helped me to take my arm back from the crocodile's mouth.

Right now it's still hard for me to accept this serious damage. I have gone through six large operations and countless small operations. At present, my left arm has no sensation, and the injury is still in the process of recovery. I still need lots of recuperative treatment—for at least two years. Although I can't work right now, I still hope that I could continue to work in the administration or management of the zoo, the treatment of animals... and so on, in the future.

June 2007

IN THE SURGEON'S OWN WORDS...

Dr Yin Chih Fu is an orthopedic surgeon at the Kaohsiung Medical University Hospital. He was one of the surgeons who worked on Chang Po-yu's arm. Ripley's tracked him down, and here is his account of what happened after the arm was severed.

The zoo had done a great job to preserve the arm. It arrived at the E.R. in a clean plastic bag in iced water. This method of preservation is critical if reattachment is to be successful. Everyone had also acted fast. The arm was in surgery just 30 minutes after it had been retrieved from the crocodile and that greatly improved its chances.

First of all, I washed the arm with copious amounts of distilled water—about 350 fl oz (10 l) of water in all—because an animal's mouth is so dirty and the risk of infection is high.

We reattached the bones first to make the arm stable. This had to be quick because we had to be able to repair the arteries as soon as possible to get oxygen to the tissue before it decayed. Even so, we had to take out some dead tissue. Then we reconnected the major veins, and afterward the nerves. The muscles were joined next, and, lastly, the skin.

Chang Po-yu had to be on high doses of antibiotics to stave off infection, but after just one month he could move his elbow and shoulder. He may need more surgery in the future, and must wait for his nerves to regenerate and muscles to heal, but eventually he should be able to grasp with his hand.

It's so important to never give up.

TASTY TOY

A pet bearded dragon, named Mushu, was treated by a veterinarian in Jacksonville, Florida, in 2007—after swallowing a 7-in (18-cm) rubber lizard.

RED SHEEP

To cheer up drivers sitting in highway traffic jams in 2007, a Scottish farmer dyed his flock of sheep red! Andrew Jack sprayed his 54-strong flock before releasing them on to the hills next to the busy M8 highway.

MATERNAL PRIDE

A lioness separately adopted three baby antelopes at Kenya's Samburu National Park over the course of a few months. Normally, a young antelope would make a delicious meal for a big cat, but this tenderhearted lioness was fiercely protective of the calves. One day, while the lioness slept, a male lion ate one of the calves. When she awoke from her slumber, the adoptive mother-of-three became grief-stricken and paced around the bush roaring in anger.

PAINTING PUPS

An art gallery in Salisbury, Maryland, staged an unusual exhibition in 2007—the artists of the exhibits were all dogs! Encouraged by dog-trainer Mary Stadelbacher, the canine Canalettos paint their masterpieces by chewing on a rubber bone with a hole drilled in the middle to hold a paintbrush. In this way they daub paint on the canvas. Each original work is signed with a black paw print in the corner and some of the doggy paintings have already sold for $350.

PIG-ASSOS

Pigs at a farm in Devon, England, paint works of art on large canvasses with their snouts and trotters. They got into art by accident, when they knocked over some tins of non-toxic paint after running amok at a craft fair.

UGLIEST DOG

After finishing second in 2006, Elwood, a Chinese Crested dog, from New Jersey, went one better in 2007 by being crowned the World's Ugliest Dog in the annual contest at Petaluma, California. With the award came a prize of $1,000. No wonder his owner Karen Quigley thinks he's cute.

SALES DOG

A dog in Pingdong City, Taiwan, is so clever that she serves customers in her owner's nut shop. The dog—named Hello—can open the refrigerator, pick up the nuts, put them on the counter, and collect money from customers. She also goes shopping by herself, waits patiently in line, and when it is her turn to be served, she puts her front paws on the counter, and gives a bag containing money and a shopping list to the waiting shopkeeper.

SNAKE SHOCK

While searching for snakes with his granddaughter in 2006, a man in Orion, Illinois, captured a two-headed bull snake.

BEST FRIENDS

In 2007, two rare Sumatran tiger cubs and two baby orangutans became inseparable friends in the nursery room of an Indonesian animal hospital. Whereas in the wild, a young orangutan would represent a tasty snack for a tiger, here the abandoned quartet regularly curled up together to sleep.

NEW TONGUE

The tongue louse, a parasite that lives on snapper fish, crawls into the mouth of a fish, eats its tongue, and then itself acts as the fish's tongue for the rest of the fish's life.

ONE OF A KIND

A calf was born in Litchfield, Nebraska, in 2007 with six legs and both male and female sex organs! The extra front and back leg extended from its pelvic area but did not reach the ground. The extra sex organs indicated that twin embryos may have fused during the animal's development.

LOBSTER LOVERS

In April 2007, a group of animal-lovers paid nearly $3,400 to buy 300 lobsters from a Maine fish market—then set them free, putting them back into the ocean.

WHALE SIZE

A blue whale's aorta—the main artery that supplies blood to the body—is so wide that a fully-grown human could swim through it.

BRAND NEW TAIL

Winter, a two-year-old bottlenose dolphin at the Clearwater Marine Aquarium in Florida, has been fitted with a prosthetic tail. The tail, which helps her to swim naturally, has a silicon sleeve that fits over her stump and a joint made of titanium. She lost her tail fin after becoming tangled in a crab trap at sea.

TWIN FREAKS

A tiger at Tianjin Zoo, China, gave birth to twin cubs in 2007—one orange, like a normal Bengal tiger, and one white. The mother is a mixed-blood tiger and it appears that, by a genetic occurence, each of her cubs has inherited her different colors.

FRENCH-SPEAKING

To strike up a rapport with their new Siberian tiger, staff at the Valley Zoo, in Edmonton, Alberta, had to find a French-speaking keeper. The tiger, named Boris, was born at a zoo in Quebec and only answers commands that are spoken in French.

SWAN LAKE

A swan on a lake in Germany has fallen in love with a plastic pedal boat. Petra the black swan circles the swan-shaped boat and makes amorous noises at it. She is so in love that when the boat didn't fly south for the winter, neither did she.

LONG LUNCH

Few birds have an appetite to match that of baby robins—they eat 14 ft (4.3 m) of earthworms every day.

PARROT LOVE

A German ornithologist has set up a dating agency—for parrots. Rita Oenhauser runs a bird sanctuary outside Berlin and has brought romance to more than 2,000 pairs of parrots. Courtship between these colorful birds can take up to three months, but once together, loved-up parrots will stay faithful to each other for life.

CONFUSED COCKATOO

Pippa, a 17-year-old cockatoo from Nuneaton, England, spent two weeks trying to hatch a bowl of chocolate Easter eggs! Her owner, Geoff Grewcock, said she saw the delicious-looking eggs on a table and climbed straight on them, because she was going through a "maternal stage." Geoff decided to let her stay on the eggs until she got off them herself—two weeks later.

GARLIC DIET

Keepers at a zoo in Shanghai, China, have been feeding their penguins garlic to help fight breathing problems and other illnesses associated with the country's rainy season. The keepers hide the cloves of garlic in the penguins' usual meals of fish.

WATCH THE BIRDIE!

A pelican resident in St. James's Park, London, England, took a radical departure from its usual diet of fish when it decided to try pigeon instead. The pelican, one of five famous pelicans in this park that lies adjacent to Buckingham Palace, was performing its usual photocall for visiting tourists when it amazed them by scooping a nearby pigeon into its beak. The hapless bird struggled in the beak for a full 20 minutes before the pelican finally swallowed it.

FISH FOOD

A black swan at Shenzhen Zoo in southern China astounds visitors by regularly feeding his fishy friends. When zookeepers bring the swan his feed, the colorful carp rush over to the bank and open their mouths. The swan then takes a morsel of food and drops it into each hungry mouth.

Cool Cat

Odin, a six-year-old white Bengal tiger who lives at the Six Flags Discovery Zoo in Vallejo, California, has no qualms about diving into water after a piece of meat thrown in by his trainer. Most cats shy away from water, but Odin loves a cool dip, especially at dinner time. Some scientists believe that because tigers evolved in eastern Asia they dislike excessive heat and may use a refreshing swim as a way to keep cool.

PET RESCUE

When a man climbed a 60-ft (18-m) pine tree to retrieve his pet cockatoo, he himself had to be rescued by a coastguard helicopter. William Hart, from Montgomery County, Texas, had scaled the tree after the bird, Geronimo, escaped from its cage.

IN A FLAP

After shooting a duck for dinner, a hunter told his wife to put it in the refrigerator, which she did. But they didn't eat the duck that night, and when the wife opened the refrigerator door two days later, the duck was still very much alive! Initially, she was shocked at seeing it look up at her, but then she took the injured bird to an animal hospital in Tallahassee, Florida, where it was treated for wing and leg wounds.

MOP MOTHER

Guzzle the goose could be a little shortsighted, because he adopted a mop as his mother while being treated at an animal care clinic in Kent, England.

PRICKLY PROBLEM

It looks like mom, it feels like mom, it even smells like mom, but it's actually a brush! However, four tiny, orphaned hedgehogs at a wildlife park in Hampshire, England, knew no better and took a fancy to the center's cleaning brush, because its bristles reminded them of their absent mother.

EXTRA FLIPPERS

A dolphin captured off the coast of Wakayama, Japan, in October 2006 had an extra set of flippers!

BATH RELIEF

After accidentally setting fire to her home in Northumberland, England, a Rottweiler puppy survived by jumping into the bath and gulping air through the plughole. Peggy had caused the fire by switching on the kitchen stove as she tried to reach her owner's chocolate birthday cake.

COW-NIVORE!

A cow in Chandpur, India, eats chickens! When 48 chickens went missing in a month, farmers suspected local dogs—until one night they saw their friendly cow, named Lal, creep in and devour several live chickens.

PURR-FECT PASSENGER

A cat in Wolverhampton, England, amazed passengers by traveling on a bus nearly every day for three months in 2007. The cat jumped on the number 331 bus, always sat at the front, and traveled for two stops before getting off near a fish-and-chip shop.

DONKEY DIAPERS

In Limuru, Kenya, the town council is trying to keep the streets clean by ordering local tradesmen to put diapers on their donkeys!

CROC COSTUME

U.S. zoologist Brady Barr studied a group of crocodiles in Tanzania up close while wearing a life-size croc costume to disguise the fact that he's a human!

CROSSBREED

A dog in a Chinese village appeared to give birth to a kitten in 2007. The first two puppies in the litter were normal but the third looked just like a cat. Vets in Jiangyan City said that it was really a puppy—it yapped like a puppy—but looked like a cat because of a gene mutation.

WHAT A HOOT!

Four tawny owl chicks at a wildlife park in Hampshire, England, were given a stuffed toy owl as their surrogate mother. To keep warm, the orphaned chicks snuggled under the wings of the fluffy toy, which had to be washed regularly because it received so much love and affection.

TALKING CAT

A cat in China is able to say his own name! The two-year-old cat, from Beijing, says his name, Agui, repeatedly when he becomes nervous or frightened.

SINGING DOG

A dog has been adding his bark to the hymn-singing at a chapel near Llanelli, Wales. Teddy the Golden Retriever goes to the chapel every Sunday with his owner Nona Rees and joins in with the rousing hymns—although he sometimes falls asleep during the sermons.

MUSICAL DOG

A dog in Xi'an, China, sings along with the ringtone on his owner's cell phone. Dangdang yaps along to the rhythm of the music whenever Mrs. Zhang's phone rings.

RUBBER LEG

A tortoise at Longleat Safari Park in Wiltshire, England, was fitted with a rubber tire and wheel to replace a leg she lost in the wild.

PIGHEADED

A piglet in Queensland, Australia, is certain he will grow into a bull! Although he was a fraction of their size and weight, Charlie the feral piglet made himself at home with two big bulls, who even let him cuddle up to them for warmth.

PARROT JOKER

An African gray parrot belonging to a New York artist has a vocabulary of 950 words and can even crack jokes! When he saw another parrot hang upside down from its perch, N'kisi squawked: "You gotta put this bird on the camera!" He also uses words in their proper context, with past, present, and future tenses.

HORSEPLAY

A dangerous horse has finally calmed down—after learning how to play soccer. Sixteen-year-old Kariba regularly used to throw off riders until horse psychologist Emma Massingale, of Devon, England, soothed the stallion's temper by getting him to kick a ball around.

BLOOD PUMP

Because of its height, a giraffe's arteries feature special valves to help pump blood all the way up to its head. Without these valves, a giraffe's heart would need to be as big as its entire body.

PORKY PUPPY

After losing its own puppies, Hui Hu, a dog in China's Chongqing municipality, found an ideal replacement—a pig. The arrangement works both ways, as the devoted pig follows its foster mother everywhere.

ACTUAL 1:1 SIZE!

BABY LOVE

A Chihuahua dog has been caring for a baby chick at a house in Guiyang City, China. Far from resenting the new pet, Huahua treated the chick as her baby and whenever it strayed too far, she would pick it up gently in her mouth and bring it back to her bed.

DOLPHIN AID

A Florida dog has been trained to sniff out dead or injured dolphins. Cloud, a female Black Labrador, works with her owner, marine biologist Chris Blankenship, who came up with the idea for a dolphin-sniffing dog after some 80 dolphins became stranded off Marathon Key in 2005. Around 30 of the animals died, mainly as a result of dehydration, but they could have been saved had they been located earlier.

WONDER WEB

A spider's web created in Texas in 2007 measured more than 200 yd (183 m) long! The web at the Lake Tawakoni State Park trapped millions of mosquitoes and was so vast that it totally engulfed seven large trees and dozens of bushes.

CHEWED CASH

A pooch named Pepper was in the doghouse in 2007 after eating $750 in cash. The dog was staying with owner Debbie Hulleman's mother in Oakdale, Minnesota, when it found a purse and chewed the contents. It spat out some money and when the family went to clean up the dog's mess outside the house, they noticed a $50 bill hanging out of one pile of poop. They gradually recovered $647 from both poop and vomit, and exchanged the cash for clean currency at a bank.

SQUIRREL ARSONISTS

Squirrels started two fires in eight days at the home of Alan Turcott, of Blue Island, Illinois—by knocking loose and chewing electrical cables.

GIANT TOAD

A huge cane toad—believed to be the biggest ever found in Australia's Northern Territory—was captured near Darwin in March 2007. Its body was 8 in (20.5 cm) long and it weighed 30½ oz (861 g). Cane toads were introduced into Australia in 1935 to control scarab beetles, a sugar-cane pest. They have since become a pest themselves, as they have spread across the country, with their toxic skin poisoning millions of native animals along the way.

THREE EYES

In 2007, a piglet at a Chinese farm was born with two faces. The mutant had one extra-large head, two mouths, and three eyes!

BLESSING IN DISGUISE

Having a leg amputated after getting it caught on a fence would be a disaster for most ducks, but not for Stumpy—because, owing to a rare mutation, he was born with four legs! In fact Stumpy, from Hampshire, England, can actually waddle much faster in pursuit of his lady-friend now that he has only one extra leg to carry.

EXTRA NOSE

A calf in Merrill, Wisconsin, was born in 2007 with two noses. Lucy has a smaller nose on the top of the first, and both noses are functional. Owner Mark Krombholz noticed the extra nose only when he fed her a bottle of milk.

FOSTER PIG

When three tiger cubs at a zoo in Guangzhou City, China, were rejected by their mother, they found an unlikely surrogate mom—a pig. Not only did the cubs gently suckle the pig's milk, they even enjoyed playing with their piglet foster brothers and sisters.

MORE PORK

A piglet born in Croatia in 2007 had a little extra of just about everything. The piglet, nicknamed Octopig, had six legs, two penises, and two anuses. He was so unusual that farmer Ivica Seic decided to keep him as a pet.

NAIL HAT

Yang Decai of Hunan, China, has been attacked so often by an angry owl that he protects himself by wearing a special hat that is fitted with nails protruding from it.

SEVEN-LEGGED LAMB

A lamb born in Christchurch, New Zealand, in 2007 was not just one in a million—it was one in several million. The lamb was born with seven legs, making it an extremely rare polydactyl, meaning many-legged animal.

FREAK CALF

When Howard Gentry saw eight legs protruding from his pregnant cow, he thought she must be giving birth to two calves. Instead, the fully grown limbs—complete with hooves—all belonged to one eight-legged calf that was stillborn at Gentry's farm in Glasgow, Kentucky, in 2007.

MOOSE ASSAULT

In March 2007, a moose rammed and downed a low-flying helicopter near Gustavus, Alaska! The animal had been shot with a tranquilizer dart, but instead of slowing down it charged the hovering helicopter, damaging the tail rotor and forcing it to the ground.

RESCUE DOG

An Italian animal-lover has trained Newfoundland dogs to jump out of helicopters and rescue people who are drowning in the sea. Ferrucio Pilenga, from Bergamo, has a team of expert canine swimmers patrolling Italy's beaches, where they have already saved a number of lives.

DOGWATCH

A 196-lb (89-kg) Newfoundland dog is the latest recruit to the lifeguards in Cornwall, England. Bilbo's training paid off when he prevented a tourist from entering dangerous currents by swimming in front of her to stop her going out any further to sea. Bilbo has his own lifeguard vest with safety messages written across it.

CAUGHT ON CAMERA!

Wondering what his pet tomcat, Mr. Lee, got up to when he went through the cat flap, Jürgen Perthold decided to find out—by fitting a tiny camera to the animal's collar.

"He goes out the whole day," says Mr. Perthold. "Sometimes he returns hungry, sometimes not, sometimes with traces of fights, and sometimes he also stays out all night. It gave me the idea to equip the cat with a camera."

At first Mr. Lee was not keen on wearing the "CatCam" but he soon got used to it, and his adventures around his home in Anderson, South Carolina, have attracted worldwide attention.

The 2½-oz (70-g) camera, which takes one photo a minute for 48 hours, has shown Mr. Lee looking longingly at bird feeders, exploring garages, hiding under cars with other cats, and even encountering a snake. It has also revealed that the tabby has a girlfriend, although he faces stiff competition from a black tom.

Mr. Lee is not the only cat to be the star of his own feline soap opera. In Los Angeles, California, Julie Peasley has fitted a lightweight camera to the collar of her gray-and-white tuxedo cat, Squeaky. Within days, she had discovered that he likes to hide in the basement of the house next door.

With CatCam, no cat's secret will ever be safe again.

ELE-VISION

For a TV documentary *Elephants: Spy in the Herd*, a miniature, remote-controlled camera was mounted on a little mobile platform and covered with dry elephant dung. The camouflage was so effective that one elephant picked up the dung cam and walked around with it still filming.

PENGUINS UNCOVERED

In 2004, scientists obtained amazing images of penguins underwater by strapping miniature cameras to the birds' backs. They found that penguins swim together with at least one other bird on about a quarter of their dives for food.

ROBOT SHARK

A robot shark was built for the U.K.'s BBC series *Smart Sharks*, containing a hidden camera that filmed sharks live in their natural habitats.

PIGEON SPIES

During the 1970s, the CIA strapped cameras—weighing as little as only a few coins—to the chests of pigeons and released the birds over enemy targets. An earlier test, with a heavier camera in the skies over Washington, D.C., failed after two days when the overburdened pigeon was forced to abandon his flight and walk home!

FLYING HIGH

TV producers strapped a miniature camera weighing almost 1 oz (25 g) to a golden eagle and were rewarded with magnificent shots as the bird soared through the air.

Please return to:

Thank you!

Mr. Lee wears his owner-made CatCam.

A bird table, but no birds...

Snakes alive!

Squeaky wearing his camera.

A Squeaky-eye view of home.

Ripley's ask Julie Peasley:

"

Why did you first fit Squeaky with a camera? Initially, I wanted to track Squeaky after he went missing for three days in 2005. Since he's an outdoor cat, I don't know where he gets off to all day. I thought that with a camera I could at least see what he is seeing and never lose track of him.

Did you make the camera yourself? No, Squeaky wears a spy cam available online for about $50.

Did he have any objections to wearing it? No, he hardly notices his new "jewelry" and, after many days wearing it, couldn't care less.

How often has Squeaky worn his camera? Five or six times. I like to put it on him first thing in the morning when he goes outside because that's when he makes his rounds of the grounds.

What is the strangest thing Squeaky has caught on camera? I found it interesting that he photographed the two-year-old child from next door looking into the apartment window.

Does Squeaky do anything sinister while out on his travels? Squeaky gets in a lot of territorial matches with other cats. If you consider squeezing through the open window of a neighbor's house sinister, he's guilty. Squeaky's brought home critters, too—a lizard, lizard tail, rat, bird, mouse, moth, grasshopper, and caterpillar.

What is your favorite picture taken by Squeaky? Hmm... it's really hard to pick a single favorite. My favorites are any that show his chin and whiskers—like a true cat-point-of-view genre of photography!

Where is Squeaky's favorite place to go? His favorite places include the upstairs balcony and any apartments that happen to have their doors open; the neighbor's yard; the neighbor's house; the neighbor's basement; under cars; in the hedge; behind the apartment building; and strolling around the carport. If his paw can open it, he goes in it.

"

It's a jungle out here!

Hmm... friend or foe?

I wonder what's in that hole.

KING HOG

A 1,050-lb (475-kg) monster hog, measuring 9 ft 4 in (2.85 m) long, was killed in Alabama in 2007—by an 11-year-old boy. Armed only with a pistol, Jamison Stone pursued the beast for three hours, shooting it eight times before finally firing the fatal bullet. The dead boar was converted into 2,800 sausages.

BUG SNIFFERS

Bill Whitstine of Safety Harbor, Florida, teaches dogs to sniff out bedbugs. One of his students, Abbey the Beagle, is such an expert that when she smells bedbugs, she sits down next to them and even points her paw at the affected area.

INFLATABLE COLLAR

Dogs in California who can't swim can wear a new inflatable dog collar. The collar—called the Float-a-Pet—fits over the dog's head and contains light-emitting diodes to help locate the animal when dusk falls.

TATTOOED FISH

Fish in Singapore are being tattooed. A tattoo laser is used to create patterns on the fish's body, including hearts, polka dots, and stripes. The tattooists maintain that the procedure does not harm the fish.

COLLIE WOBBLE

Kyle, a 14-year-old collie, who is partially blind and is also hard of hearing, survived a 50-ft (15-m) plunge at a Scottish waterfall—called Dog Falls. Despite being the place of Kyle's misfortune, the spot actually gets its name because the water falls in the shape of a dog's leg.

FISHING BATS

Whereas most bats prefer to eat insects, the bulldog bat from Central and South America is an accomplished fisherman. It trails its extra-long legs in the water and grabs fish with its huge hooked claws.

MONKEY BUSINESS

Monkeys are trained to assist in Thailand's coconut industry, because a single monkey can climb through the trees and easily pick hundreds of coconuts a day.

DISTINCTIVE BULL

The main attraction at a zoo in Guangzhou City, China, is a five-legged bull. The animal looks perfectly normal—apart from an extra leg growing on its back.

DINNER DATE

A wolf captured in Albania in 2007 became best friends with its dinner! A donkey was put in the wolf's cage as a prospective meal, but instead of hunting it down and eating it, the wolf made the donkey its friend.

TABLE MANNERS

Gorillas have table manners. A conservation group tracking western lowland gorillas in Africa has discovered that, after eating, they politely wipe their hands and faces with leaves—in exactly the same way that humans use table napkins.

HIGHWAY ROBBERY

In 2007, motorists in the Orissa state of India reported that a wild elephant refused to let their vehicles pass unless they gave him food. The elephant stood in the highway, forcing vehicles to stop, and moved aside only when fed with vegetables or bananas.

HEROIC CHIHUAHUA

A tiny Chihuahua saved the life of a one-year-old boy who was attacked by a rattlesnake. Booker West was playing in his grandparents' backyard in Masonville, Colorado, when the snake lunged, but Zoey the Chihuahua jumped in the way and took the bites. Happily, the brave dog survived.

BUSY BURROWS

In 1900, a single prairie-dog town in Texas covered 25,000 sq mi (64,750 sq km) and had a whopping estimated population of 400 million animals!

LION KISS

The owner of an animal refuge in Cali, Colombia, is on kissing terms with a fully grown lion! Ana Julia Torres rescued Jupiter the lion from a traveling circus seven years ago and now he repays her kindness by tenderly hugging her with his giant paws through the bars of his cage, and by planting a kiss on her mouth.

LONG EARS

Nipper's Geronimo, an English lop-eared rabbit owned by the Nipper family of Bakersfield, California, has ears that are more than 2½ ft (76 cm) long.

ZOO CLOWN

A German zoo has hired a clown to cheer up its gorillas, orangutans, and chimpanzees. Zoo chiefs hired local entertainer Christina Peter to keep the animals amused after research found that apes tended to become sick or aggressive when bored.

LANGUAGE BARRIERS

When Milo the Jack Russell terrier became trapped in a drain in England in 2007, its rescuers had to talk French to it because the dog used to belong to a family in France and it couldn't understand a word of English.

Ripley's research . . . .

Reports of winged cats have occurred sporadically over the years.

In 1966, a winged cat was said to be swooping down on farm animals at Alfred, Ontario, Canada. The animal was shot dead, and when exhumed, its "wings" were found to be nothing more than matted fur. It also had rabies, which accounted for its bizarre behavior.

The owner of the cat in China (right) is convinced that her pet sprouted wings after being harassed by female cats in heat. However, the cause is more likely to be either a genetic mutation or a rare hereditary skin condition called Feline Cutaneous Asthenia. This ailment results in the skin on the cat's shoulders, back, and haunches becoming abnormally elastic and forming pendulous, wing-like folds or flaps that sometimes contain muscle fibers.

Winged Cat

A cat in China has grown wings! Granny Feng of Xianyang City, was amazed to see what started out as two bumps on her cat's back grow into 4-in-long (10-cm) wing-like sprouts in less than a month in 2007. She said that the wings, which contain bones, make her pet look like a "cat angel."

PARROT LOOKOUTS

During World War I, parrots were kept on the Eiffel Tower in Paris, France, to warn of approaching German aircraft. Owing to their acute sense of hearing, the birds could detect enemy planes long before they came into the range of human lookouts.

SERIAL SWALLOWER

Taffy the Springer Spaniel needed an operation in 2007 after swallowing his 40th pair of underpants. The 18-month-old dog, which belongs to vet Eubie Saayman of Staffordshire, England, has also gulped down 300 socks, destroyed 15 pairs of shoes, and once ate the keys to the family's Mercedes car.

WEIGHTY WHIPPET

Wendy, a dog from Central Saanich, Canada, has a mutated set of muscular growth genes, making her "double-muscled" and twice the weight of an average Whippet.

NEW SPECIES

Scientists have discovered that hammerhead sharks can reproduce without having sex. The news was announced following studies of a female shark at Henry Doorly Zoo in Nebraska that gave birth to a pup in 2001 despite having had no contact with a male.

BEFORE

AFTER

BALL OF WOOL

Victa the sheep had a woolly coat that was five times his own body weight. Having not been sheared for up to three years at his backyard home in Melbourne, Australia, his wool had become so thick that he had problems bending down to eat. Luckily, Victa was rescued by animal protection officers and given a long-overdue shearing, after which he perked up considerably.

TWIN TURTLE

An aquarium in East Norriton, Pennsylvania, displayed a red-eared slider turtle that had two heads. The reptilian oddity had a pair of front feet on each side, but just one pair of back feet and only one tail.

Ripley's research

This two-headed turtle in Pennsylvania is actually a pair of conjoined red-eared slider twins. Whether in humans or animals, conjoined twins are caused when the developing embryo starts to split into identical twins but the process stops before it is complete, leaving a partially separated egg.

Ripley's research....

With a zebra for a father and a horse for a mother, Eclyse is living proof that children inherit the genes of both parents. Most zebra-horse crossbreeds have stripes across their entire body but, by a freak of nature, Eclyse is only partially striped.

IT'S A ZORSE!

Visitors to a German safari park don't know quite what to make of Eclyse, its star attraction. Her head and rear are striped like a zebra, but the rest of her body and legs are snow white. The reason she looks so strange is that she's a "zorse," her father being a zebra and her mother a horse. While most zebra–horse crossbreeds sport stripes across their entire body, Eclyse has only two striped patches, giving her a truly unique appearance.

PAW AND ORDER

Alex, a 13-year-old Golden Retriever of Memphis, Tennessee, had an attorney appointed to represent his interests in a custody battle after his owner's death!

HAPPY HOMECOMING

Twenty months after disappearing from the Tighe family residence in Hallam, Nebraska, during a tornado, Harley the cat suddenly returned home in January 2006.

MUTANT MICE

Mutant mice created by scientists in Philadelphia, Pennsylvania, can grow back their toes and limbs and repair their severed spinal cords.

ELEPHANT'S BUZZWORD

Despite a huge difference in size and even though their skin is believed to be too thick for them to feel pain from a sting, African elephants are frightened by bees. Researchers have found that entire herds will steer clear of the sound of buzzing bees, and if bees get up elephants' trunks the animals go berserk.

LADYBUG'S BALL

A New York City apartment complex released 720,000 ladybugs onto its premises in October 2007 to help clear the grounds of parasitic insects.

BACK TO LIFE

A hamster in Dagenham, England, was miraculously brought back to life after being accidentally cooked. Christmas the hamster was charred when the oven on which his cage was standing was turned on by mistake. When firefighters arrived, he was lying on his back with his legs in the air and his tongue hanging out, but after some oxygen, a rub of his tummy, and a few sips of juice, amazingly he was resuscitated.

PAMPERED PET

A wealthy New York hotel magnate left $12 million in her will to her dog. Leona Helmsley doted on her Maltese terrier, Trouble, and also stipulated that when the dog dies, it should be buried next to her.

HIDING PLACE

A New Jersey cat survived a house fire in 2007 by hiding in the furniture. The owners of the house in West Orange thought the cat must have perished, but were amazed to find their pet had wedged itself into the couch.

MOUTH-TO-MOUTH

A man saved the life of his bulldog puppy by resuscitating her after she had fallen into an icy lake while chasing ducks and geese. The puppy, named Lucy, had a blue face and paws by the time Randy Gurchin pulled her from the wintry water in Sarpy County, Nebraska, but he revived her by closing her mouth, placing his mouth over her nose, and then breathing into her lungs while pushing on her chest.

JUMBO JOB

City officials of Barisal, Bangladesh, hired circus elephants to help them to demolish illegal buildings in March 2007. With a lack of mechanical demolition tools at their disposal, officials called in the elephants, who demolished the buildings in minutes.

PATTERN CONTROL

Female North American side-blotched lizards control the patterns of their offspring's camouflage by releasing different amounts of hormones into their eggs.

MYNAH OFFENCE

A mynah bird was placed in solitary confinement at a zoo in Changsha, China, after being rude to visitors. After calling tourists stupid and ugly, eight-year-old Mimi had to stay in a darkened cage for 15 days and listen to recordings of polite conversation in an attempt to improve her behavior and language.

FOOD CYCLE

Leaf-cutting ants from South America actually grow their own food. They forage for plants and leaves, carry them home and then chew the pieces into a form of compost, which they proceed to spread on the floors of their underground chambers. Eventually, fungus grows on the compost and is eaten by the ants.

EXPERT MIMICS

Australia's lyrebirds mimic a huge range of natural and artificial sounds including other birds, dog barks, car alarms, musical instruments, and even revving chainsaws!

Dances with Buffalo

Some families keep dogs, others keep cats, but the Bridges family of Quinlan, Texas, have a truly unusual pet—a 1300-lb (590-kg) buffalo named Wildthing.

Wildthing has his own room in the house, where he eats and sleeps, and is so tame that he follows his master, R.C. Bridges, everywhere and even used to dance with him. They are best friends and, when Wildthing turned two in 2007, the family staged a birthday party in his room,

draping it in ribbons and making a cake of feed and icing shaped like a buffalo patty, topped with a candle.

R.C., a cowboy since childhood, started raising the baby buffalo in 2005. Helped by his son Lloyd, he "halter broke" the young bull even though Wildthing could kick and push with the strength of a fully grown animal. Since then, R.C. has taught Wildthing to pull a plow, and also a chariot on which he takes the family for rides. Wildthing will happily pull R.C.'s daughter

Taylor along on a sleigh and another son Will has learned to ski behind him.

"Wildthing has so much energy and personality," says R.C.'s wife Sherron, who reveals that the buffalo likes to play with a basketball and to take baths. Unfortunately, Wildthing has become too big to dance with—and he still has another 700–800 lb (315–360 kg) to gain before he's fully grown.

R.C. Bridges began training Wildthing when the buffalo was two months old.

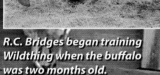

Wildthing tucks into a birthday meal in his own special living quarters.

When R.C. and Sherron renewed their wedding vows in 2006, they had their wedding photos retaken with Wildthing as best man.

Wildthing spends much of his day in the house, but he also has a pen in the yard.

Wildthing rarely leaves R.C.'s side. Even when R.C. sits down, Wildthing will lie down next to him.

In Sherron Bridges' own words...

"When we're away from the house for a couple of hours or more, Wildthing will call out to the truck as we pull into the driveway. You'll hear him grunting and he'll run and bounce with excitement because he sees R.C. is in the truck. Grunting is his call to R.C. to come out and feed or brush and scratch him. As long as Wildthing can see R.C., he is just fine.

Wildthing can get his feelings hurt by R.C. telling him he can't come in the house. Wildthing will then pout by walking away or even going to lie down. We won't let him in the house if he is all wound up, because he could hurt you just by slinging his head around, even if it's just to warn you to leave him alone. If R.C. has to tell him off for scratching on the side of the house or horning at the windows, he pouts.

Healthy buffalo usually live for about 40 years. We would be lost if anything happened to Wildthing, and Wildthing would be lost if anything happened to R.C."

The Bridges family with their big baby, Wildthing. He still has a lot more growing to do.

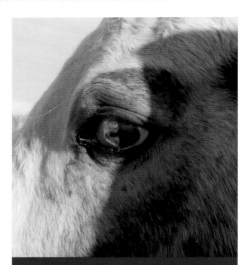

COLOR SPLIT

Peavey, a horse belonging to Ann Huth-Fretz of Tiffin, Ohio, has a two-tone eye, with the colors split straight down the middle!

SNAKE SLAIN

When a deadly viper slithered into the intensive care ward of a Croatian hospital, 80-year-old patient Miko Vukovic, who was recovering from heart surgery, jumped from his bed and beat the snake to death with his walking stick.

FIRE RESCUE

Jango, a Golden Retriever from Trail, British Columbia, Canada, saved his family from a fire by barking as the house filled with smoke. The dog then continued to bark to help the Unger family navigate their way to safety through the flames.

CARING CAT

A nine-year-old boy with Type 1 diabetes was saved from having a possible seizure by the attention of his cat. Mel-O climbed the ladder to Alex Rose's loft bed in his home in Morinville, Alberta, Canada, walked on his chest, swatted his face, and purred in his ear until he got out of bed. When he went to his mother, his glucose levels were found to be dangerously low. Nobody knows how the cat managed to sense low blood sugar.

MILK BOOST

Romanian farmers have boosted milk production by playing music to their cows. Cowhands have set up CD players in the stables, and the music relaxes the animals so much that they even come in alone from the fields just to listen to more tunes.

CLIFF ORDEAL

A dog survived for two weeks on a ledge 100 ft (30 m) high in Devon, England, in 2007, by eating a dead bird and drinking from a waterfall. Bush the Staffordshire bull terrier had disappeared from his owner's sight when he ran over the edge of the cliff in pursuit of a deer.

JELLYFISH INVASION

In November 2007, billions of jellyfish washed into a salmon farm in Northern Ireland killing every one of the 100,000-plus fish.

HIDDEN PASSENGER

Arriving in her hotel room in Niagara, Ontario, Canada, after a two-hour flight from New Brunswick, Mary Martell opened her suitcase—and was amazed to find her cat Ginger inside. The cat had jumped into the case while Mrs. Martell was packing and had even escaped detection by airport security.

DOLPHIN RESCUE

Dolphins rescued surfer Todd Endris from a deadly shark attack off the coast of Monterey, California, by driving the shark away and surrounding the 24-year-old until help could arrive. Endris had been attacked by a 15-ft-long (4.5-m) great white shark, which had rammed him three times and was about to swallow his right leg when he managed to free himself. As the shark moved in for the kill, the bottlenose dolphins swam to his rescue and managed to keep the predator at bay. Talking to journalists, Endris described the rescue as "truly a miracle."

FISHING SETTER

A Croatian fisherman decided to sell his dog because it kept embarrassing him by catching more fish than he did. Whereas Slobodan Paparella reels in the occasional fish while out with his pals, his Irish setter Lipi would leap into the water and catch dozens.

TWO-FACED

A two-faced calf, named Star, was born recently at a dairy farm in Rural Retreat, Virginia. The curious creature had three sets of teeth, two lower jaws, and two tongues, but only one mouth. It also had two noses with separate airways, but only a single eye socket with two eyes in it!

ODD EYES

A two-year-old cat in Riyadh, Saudi Arabia, has different-colored eyes—one brown and one blue. Appropriately, the cat is a mix of Persian and Siamese.

DOGGY DUDE

The owner of a leather goods shop in Suzhou City, China, dresses her pet dog in T-shirt and jeans to welcome customers. The dog greets them with a friendly bark and bows courteously when they leave.

LION CHASE

Drivers in Wakefield, Ohio, are used to their cars being chased by dogs, but in November 2007 they were hotly pursued by a lion. Pike County sheriff's deputies responded to a 911 call of a lion "attacking" vehicles on U.S. 23 after the 550-lb (250-kg) beast, named Lambert, had escaped from its pen.

DOG SCENT

A firm in London, England, has launched a perfume for dogs. Petite Amande, which features blackcurrant, mimosa, vanilla, and almond, is designed to appeal to the canine nose and comes with a matching shampoo.

Troubled Triplets

Triplet puppies were born in Virginia in 2007, without any front legs—the first case of its kind in the world. Yet with the aid of daily physiotherapy at a New York animal shelter to strengthen their muscles, the brave little Chihuahuas were soon getting around by standing upright and hopping on their back legs.

JAR ORDEAL

A cat survived for 19 days with a peanut-butter jar stuck on her head. Thin and weak through lack of food, the feral cat was saved by the Cain family of Bartlett, Tennessee, who used oil to pry the jar off the animal's head and then nursed her back to health.

STRONG LEGS

Believe it or not, one leg of a mosquito can support 23 times the insect's weight—while standing on water.

PIE SNATCH

The 2007 World Pie Eating Championships were thrown into disarray after the organizer's dog woofed the pies. While Dave Williams, who won the title in 1995, was looking after the precious tournament pies at his home in Lancashire, England, his pet dog Charlie managed to sneak in and eat at least ten of them.

Ripley's research . . . .

TWO-FACED: Animals usually form two heads or faces because of a condition called axial bifurcation—an abnormality that occurs when an embryo is damaged in the womb. This can result in the formation of a lesion, causing some parts to develop in duplicate. Polycephalic (two-headed) animals rarely live very long.

TROUBLED TRIPLETS: The birth defects in the Chihuahuas below are thought to have been caused by excessive inbreeding—breeding between close relatives. Breeders of domestic animals use inbreeding to maintain desirable characteristics within the breed, but it can sometimes lead to genetic disorders and physical defects. While three of the puppies were born without front legs, the other two in the litter were normal.

COLOR SPLIT & ODD EYES: The condition to describe one eye that is a different color from the other is called heterochromia. It is caused by an excess or lack of pigment within the eye and can be inherited or acquired through mutation, disease, or injury. The rarer condition of sectoral heterochromia produces different colors within the same eye.

Hair-raising Yarn!

Victoria Pettigrew hated throwing away the hair from her pet Chow's brush after grooming. So one day she decided to spin it into yarn. Her idea has prompted pet lovers across the United States to wear their pets' hair with pride—in bed, to stores, and even to the beach.

When Victoria's beloved 16-year-old Lhasa Apso dog, Karly, died in 2001, she spun her fur and knitted it into a small scarf. Now customers send hair from their dogs and cats to her company—VIP Fibers of Denton, Texas—and she spins it into yarn before sending it back to them as maybe a pair of mittens, a scarf, a blanket, a pillow, or, for the more daring, a fun-fur bikini. Such items are proving to be popular keepsakes with which owners can remember their adored pets.

Dog fur is up to 80 percent warmer than sheep's wool, but has to be thoroughly cleaned so that when the yarn gets wet, it does not smell like a wet dog. First the hair is washed in shampoo, then it is put through a process that removes the enzymes that cause odor, and finally it is soaked in softener and conditioner.

Victoria also spins yarn from alpacas, rabbits, horses, and even hamsters, although it may need several years' fur collection to create a hamster blanket!

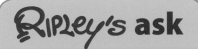

From raw fibers through being spun into finished yarn, the pet hair undergoes a thorough cleaning process.

Victoria's friend Gary used her company to make his hat from his cat Teddie's hair.

Victoria wears a sweater made from hair from her dog BooBoo Bear.

Ripley's ask

" **How much yarn has VIP Fibers spun in its seven-year history?** To date, we have spun 1,531,926 yards of pet yarn. We have created hundreds, if not thousands, of finished Furever Keepsakes from a portion of this yarn.

Do you make every item personally? No, in the past the company has had up to four employees. Currently, we have one. In addition, my husband Stephen comes in to card fiber on a part-time basis—I perform all other tasks.

How much fur does it take to make a sweater? General rule of thumb is 2½ lb (1.1 kg) of raw fiber for a basic, large sweater. However, we do not recommend making an entire sweater from 100 percent "canine cashmere," as dog hair is up to 80 percent warmer than wool. A sweater constructed completely from dog hair would simply be too warm to wear.

Is there any specific type of animal fur you like to work with? My favorite fiber is any from a beloved and spoiled pet! They have the nicest fur!

What is the weirdest thing you have been asked to make? We were asked to make three dog-fur bikinis for a TV show last year.

What is the most peculiar animal fur you have worked with? Fur belonging to a Bengal tiger. "

DOGGIE DUDES

Four-legged surfing dudes get the chance to shine at the annual Loews Coronado Bay Resort Surf Dog Competition in California. Forty-seven canines took part in 2007, the contest being divided into two sections—the first purely for dogs and the second for dogs and humans surfing together on the same board at the same time. Prizes included a gourmet doggie room service meal at the resort and a basket filled with dog treats.

TIGER ATTACK

A stray dog had a lucky escape in January 2008 when it wandered into the tiger pit at the Memphis Zoo in Memphis, Tennessee. The 50-lb (23-kg) female retriever-mix jumped over a railing and a wall before swimming across a moat to the center of the enclosure, where it was attacked by a 225-lb (100-kg) Sumatran tiger. Seeing the incident, zoo workers used fireworks and air horns to distract the tiger and, despite being held in the tiger's grasp for several minutes, the dog escaped with nothing worse than puncture wounds to its neck and shoulders.

TOO HEAVY

Young gannets are fed so much fish that they are unable to fly. On leaving the nest, they have to fast for a couple of weeks until they are light enough to get airborne.

AUTO SHEEP

Too old to be able to walk alongside his animals, a resourceful Greek shepherd named George Zokos has trained his flock of sheep to follow his car instead.

FAKE BURIALS

Animal experts have discovered that gray squirrels fake food burials in order to confuse their rivals if they think they are being watched. To protect their winter food stocks from potential thieves, squirrels put on an elaborate show of burying non-existent nuts and seeds, even covering them over with soil to dupe any thieving onlookers.

ACTUAL 1:1 SIZE!

Burley Beetle

There is a beetle that is longer than an adult human hand! The titan beetle (or giant long-horned beetle) of the Amazon rainforest can grow up to 8 in (21 cm) in length, including its antennae. Its mandibles are so strong that they can snap pencils in half and cut into human flesh.

Enter the Vault

MAD MARKINGS

Pete the monocled dog was owned by Harry Lucenay in the 1930s. His startling natural markings helped launch his movie career—Pete was a star in the popular "Our Gang" short films of the 1930s.

CONJOINED CALVES

In March 1932, Dr. M.T. Cook of Cumberland, Kentucky, delivered these live conjoined calves that belonged to Gravil Cornett, of Dione, Kentucky.

◄ FASHIONABLE FELINE

Mickey was a Maltese cat who was given a whole new wardrobe every Easter by his owner, New Yorker Joseph Orlando. This outfit, from his 1950 collection, features puffed sleeves and a fetching hat.

DOG STAR

In 1950, the Horden twins of East Falls, Pennsylvania, were the proud owners of a black dog named Rip who had a perfect white-star marking on his chest.

SKILLFUL SHEEP

In the early 1930s, Clarence Bosworth of Cayton, California, was the proud owner of a sheep that could walk on its front legs.

HORNED ROOSTER

This rooster, owned by Jesse Parker of Dequeen, Arkansas, in the early 1930s had two horns sticking out of the top of its head.

FAT CAT

This 1935 photograph shows a cat of considerable proportions that was owned by A.M. Turner of Wimbledon, England. The fat feline weighed a whopping 35 lb (16 kg).

RAT TRAP

In the cold winter of 1934, C.H. Watson of Cuba, New York, found this rat that had frozen to death when it made the fatal mistake of licking an icy iron bar.

BEAKLESS BIRD

This chicken with no beak was owned by the Milbank Creamery in South Dakota in 1932.

TWO-NOSED DOG

This setter with two noses was owned by John Glenn of Benton, Arkansas, in the 1940s.

Ted, a four-year-old terrier owned by Bill Vandever from Tulsa, Oklahoma, is seen here climbing 10 ft (3 m) up a tree to retrieve his ball in 1944.

CANINE CLIMBERS

Elmer, a dog from Connecticut, used to report for duty at his job working for a construction firm. He would regularly climb the ladders onto the roofs of buildings in the mid-1950s.

NAIL SCULPTOR

These sculptures of a life-size moose and bison are made entirely from nails. They are the work of artist Bill Secunda from Butler, Pennsylvania, who specializes in creating metal creatures. The moose is made from 95,000 welded nails, weighs 1,800 lb (815 kg), stands 7½ ft (2.3 m) tall, 12 ft (3.6 m) long, and has antlers that are almost 9 ft (2.7 m) wide. The bison, made from 30,000 cut and framing nails, weighs 1,100 lb (500 kg) and is 6 ft (1.8 m) tall, 3 ft (90 cm) wide, and 8 ft (2.4 m) long.

HUNGRY WOLF

In December 2007, customers at a crowded bar in Villetta Barrea, Italy, were shocked when a wolf strolled in, ate a steak sandwich, and walked out again. The hungry beast, which came from the nearby Abruzzo National Park, had been driven to drastic measures by a spell of cold weather.

COURAGEOUS KITTENS

An elderly Chinese woman was saved in 2006 when eight family cats fought off a giant cobra that was trying to slither into her bed. As the deadly 6-ft (1.8-m) serpent made its way across the floor, the cats surrounded it, the mother cat stamping on the snake's head and the seven kittens biting its body and dragging it out of the house. As the cats pinned the snake to the ground, the old woman's son beat it to death.

HEAD STUCK

A cat in Cambridgeshire, England, got its head stuck after trying to pull a mouse out of a jelly jar. The cat was found wandering next to a road with the jar on its head and the mouse just in front of its nose. The cat eventually freed both itself and the mouse by smashing the jar.

RAPID GROWTH

In just two weeks, the monarch butterfly caterpillar grows to 2,700 times its birth weight. If a 7-lb (3.2-kg) human baby gained weight at the same rate, it would weigh more than nine tons.

NO SWEAT!

Camels can lose up to 30 percent of their body weight in perspiration and still survive. By contrast, a human would die of heat shock after sweating away just 12 percent of his or her body weight.

PIG COUNTRY

There are more wild pigs than people in Australia, which has a population of 21 million people and 23 million feral pigs.

GIANT RAT

In 2007, researchers in a remote jungle in Indonesia discovered a hitherto unknown species of giant rat that is about five times the size of a typical city rat and has no fear of humans. A 2006 expedition to the same stretch of jungle had uncovered dozens of new species of palms and butterflies.

PET FOX

Instead of behaving like a wild animal, Cropper the fox lives indoors with Mike Towler and his family, eats from a dog bowl, and curls up with the household cats. Towler from the town of Tunbridge Wells in Kent, England, tamed Cropper over a period of several months after the fox contracted a memory-damaging disease that left him unable to make a home or recognize prey.

BIG BONE

Walking along the beach in the village of Dunwich in Suffolk, England, in 2007, Daisy the miniature wire-haired Dachshund stumbled across a bone that was as big as herself. The bone—measuring 13 in (33 cm) long and weighing 8 lb (3.6 kg)—was a fossilized thigh section of a two-million-year-old mammoth.

TODDLER SAVED

When R.C., a German Shepherd–Husky cross, discovered two-year-old Vincent Rhodey outdoors in the freezing cold wearing only a T-shirt, he instinctively sat on the youngster and saved him from hypothermia. The boy had strayed from his home in Canonsburg, Pennsylvania, but R.C. curled up with him for nearly an hour to keep him warm until they were both found.

MONSTER PYTHON

Fluffy, a huge python bought in 2008 by Columbus Zoo, Ohio, has a body as long as a small truck and as thick as a telegraph pole. Fed 10 lb (4.5 kg) of rabbits a week, Fluffy is 22 ft (7 m) long and is thought to be one of the biggest snakes currently in captivity.

LIVING DEAD

When Gan Shugen of Chengdu, China, went to cook a chicken that he had kept in a freezer for two days, he was shocked to find it was still alive. The bird—a gift from a relative—was wrapped in a thick plastic bag with its legs tied, leading Gan to assume it was dead. Instead, despite 48 hours in sub-zero temperatures, it poked its head out of the bag and was soon able to stand.

DEEP BREATH

Armadillos can hold their breath for up to six minutes. That is how they are able to poke their noses deep into the ground in search of insects.

BLUE HAZE

The wings of the *Morpho sulkowskyi* butterfly have a self-cleaning texture that repels water and reflects light to give it a bright blue appearance.

LOUD HOWL

The scream of a howler monkey can be heard up to 5 mi (8 km) away. It is so noisy that the sound of a family of howlers traveling through the forest has been mistaken for a thunderstorm.

POOCH HOOCH

Pet-shop owner Gerrie Berendsen of Zelhem, the Netherlands, has devised a new beer—for dogs. The nonalcoholic brew is made from a mix of beef extract and malt.

BUSHY-TAILED BURGLAR

A squirrel with a sweet tooth raided a Finnish grocery store at least twice a day to steal chocolate candy eggs with a toy inside. The manager of the store in Jyvaskyla said the squirrel always carefully removed the foil wrapping, ate the chocolate, and left carrying the toy.

THE STING

Octopuses have been known to remove the stings from captured jellyfish and attach them to their own tentacles to use as an added weapon.

SKINNY PIG

The latest designer pet is the skinny pig, a hairless breed of guinea pig first created for laboratory testing 30 years ago. As they are naked, skinny pigs need to be kept warm on cold days, but will also burn if left in the sun for too long without protective suncream.

SWOLLEN TONGUE
A dead humpback whale was found washed up on the coast of Alaska in 2007 with its tongue swollen to the size of a car. Scientists investigating the death of the whale think that a collision forced air into its tongue and caused it to swell.

ARTISTIC GORILLAS
Gorillas at Franklin Park Zoo in Boston, Massachusetts, are keen finger-painters. Keepers at the zoo claim that the finger-painting helps to keep the apes intellectually stimulated; and it earns them money too—one of their artworks sold for a whopping $10,000!

KITTEN SAVIOR
Zacheri Richardson-Leitman of Cairns, Queensland, Australia, had time to rescue his whole family from a blaze, despite being in bed asleep when his mattress caught fire. How did he do it? His ten-week-old kitten scratched at his face to wake him up and alert him to his burning bed.

RUNT OF THE LITTER
Part of a litter of 14 in Gansu, China, this piglet was born with one eye, four eyeballs, and a long nose that made it look like a baby elephant.

MYTHICAL BEAST?

When Phylis Canion found a strange animal dead outside her Cuero, Texas, ranch in August 2007, she thought it was a chupacabra, the mysterious beast blamed for killing 30 of her chickens. DNA tests revealed that the beast was part coyote (on the maternal side) and part Mexican wolf (on the paternal side).

Ripley's research

What is a chupacabra?

Nobody knows for sure whether the chupacabra is an undiscovered breed of animal or just a myth. The chupacabra gets its name, which is Spanish for "goat sucker", from its habit of attacking and drinking the blood of livestock. Dozens of sightings of the beast have been reported from Maine to Chile. Descriptions of it vary from a hairless doglike creature to a spiny reptile that hops like a kangaroo and has red glowing eyes. Some witnesses claim that it has wings. In 2006, a farmer from Coleman, Texas, killed a weird creature that mauled some of his chickens and turkeys. It was described as a cross between a dog, a rat, and a kangaroo, but was thrown out with the trash. Around the same time an evil-looking, rodent-like creature with fangs was found dead alongside a road near Turner, Maine, but the carcass was picked clean by vultures before anyone could examine it. In 2004, a rancher near San Antonio, Texas, killed a hairless doglike creature that was attacking his livestock. The Elmendorf Beast, as it became known, was in fact a coyote.

NEW SPECIES

Scientists in Indonesia identified 20 new species of sharks and rays during a five-year survey of catches at Indonesian fish markets.

HEROIC HOUND

A Golden Labrador saved a woman's life in 2007 by giving her the Heimlich maneuver. Debbie Parkhurst of Cecil County, Maryland, was eating an apple when a piece got stuck in her throat. Her choking alerted her two-year-old dog Toby, who stood on his hind feet, put his front paws on her shoulders, pushed her to the ground, and began jumping up and down on her chest, an action that dislodged the apple from her windpipe. As soon as Mrs. Parkhurst started breathing again, the dog stopped jumping and began licking its owner's face to stop her from passing out.

CAT COMFORT

A New York couple paid out more than $3,000 in taxi fares for the journey to their new home in Arizona—just so their two cats could travel in comfort. Pensioners Betty and Bob Matas were afraid that their pets would suffer in the cargo hold of a plane, so they opted to make the 2,500-mi (4,025-km) journey to the Southwest by cab, with the cats resting comfortably in carpet-lined cages in the back of the vehicle.

FELINE STOWAWAY

Taking delivery of a consignment of motorcycle helmets from China, the owner of a shop in North Carolina opened the box to find a cat inside. The animal had managed to chew its way into the cardboard box somewhere in Shanghai and had somehow survived the 35-day sea voyage despite being trapped in a cargo crate without food or water.

ODD COUPLE

When Mozambique was flooded in 2002, a dog from the village of Caia became firm friends with a wild monkey. The two played together and the dog even let the monkey ride on its back.

DUNG GIFT

The Valley Zoo, at Edmonton, Alberta, Canada, sells an unusual line in Mothers' Day presents—20-lb (9-kg) bags of composted animal dung. The zoo says the compost—made from the droppings of elephants, zebras, camels, and antelopes—is the ideal gift for keen gardeners.

NURSING HOME

Japan has opened a nursing home for dogs! Owners pay to keep their aging pets at the home in Tochigi, where the dogs have veterinary care as well as a team of puppies to play with in order to help them keep fit.

HEART SHAPE

A Chihuahua puppy was born in Japan in 2007 with a large heart-shaped pattern on his coat. Shop-owner Emiko Sakurada said the dog, named Heart-kun, was unique.

PIG WEDDING

Two pet pigs were married in Taiwan in 2007 with the blessing of a church priest. Farm owner Xu Wenchuan decided to reward his male pig, Xu Fuge, for all the hard work he does welcoming guests at the farm restaurant, and advertised for a suitable bride. Two parrots acted as bridesmaid and groomsman at the ceremony.

FOWL PLAY

Two chickens in China have become addicted to playing soccer! Owner Mrs. Zhang found an abandoned football and decided to give it to the competitive bantams for fun. Since then they play with the ball every day and can even perform sliding tackles.

ELEPHANTS' PICNIC

In 2007, two elephants escaped from a circus and went strolling around the town of Newmarket, Ontario, Canada, eating grass and trees in neighboring gardens during the early hours of the morning. A woman who saw them couldn't believe her eyes!

SWALLOWED TEETH

A Jack Russell terrier was rushed into surgery in 2007—after eating his owner's false teeth! The dog, who was named Desmond, swallowed Marjorie Johnson's dentures one morning while she was in the bathroom at her home near Newcastle, England. Veterinarians had to open up the dog's stomach to retrieve the teeth in an operation that lasted three hours.

STUCK DUCK

Eighteen firefighters, three fire trucks, a Land Rover four-wheel drive, and a rescue boat were used in a three-hour rescue to save a trapped duck near Birmingham, England. As crews raced to the scene from 35 mi (56 km) away, residents feared a child had drowned, but it turned out the casualty was Daffy, a white Aylesbury duck who was stranded in a drainage tunnel.

CAT-LOVING DOG

Ginny, a Schnauzer–Siberian husky cross, rescued more than 1,000 cats in her lifetime. She had the unique accolade, for a dog, of being named Cat of the Year at the 1998 Westchester Cat Show, in New York. When she died in 2005, at the ripe old age of 17, her memorial service was attended by 300 cats. Her owner, Philip Gonzalez from Long Beach, New York, never trained her—she just knew instinctively when a cat was in trouble. "Ginny loved cats," he said. "And cats loved Ginny."

MUMMIFIED DOG

In 1980, a mummified dog was found lodged 20 ft (6 m) above ground in a tree near the Georgia–Alabama state line. The hollow tree created perfect conditions for the animal to be preserved some 20 years after its death. The dog became so popular that it was later given its own name—Stuckie.

ACKNOWLEDGMENTS

COVER (l) Rick Murphy, Six Flags Discovery Kingdom; (t/r) Michael Steve Bean, (b/r) Sherron Bridges; 4 Rick Murphy, Six Flags Discovery Kingdom; 6 (t) Steve Chen/AP/PA Photos; 7 Reuters/Frank Lin; 8 Richard Austin/Rex Features; 9 (t) Ben Margot/AP/PA Photos, (r) Reuters/Yuriko Nakao; 10 (b/l, b/c) Cathal McNaughton/PA Archive/PA Photos, (b/r, c/r, c/r, t/r) Rick Murphy, Six Flags Discovery Kingdom; 11 (sp) Robyn Beck/AFP/Getty Images, (t/r) CNImaging/Photoshot; 12 (t) Piers Morgan/Rex Features, (c) Simon Czapp/Rex Features, (b) Chris Balcombe/Rex Features; 13 (t) S Chalker/Newspix/Rex Features, (b) ChinaFotoPress/Zhong Zhibing/Photocome/PA Photos; 14 Frogwatch (North)/Getty Images; 15 (t) Reuters/Alessandro Garofalo, (b) Colin Shepherd/Rex Features; 16 (b/l, b/c, b/r) Mr.Lee/J.Perthold; 17 (b/l, b/c, b/r) Mr.Lee/J.Perthold, (c, t) Julie Peasley; 18 (t) Mike Stone, (b) Inaldo Perez/AP/PA Photos; 19 Camera Press/ChinaFotoPress; 20 (t, c) Newspix/Rex Features, (b) Matt Rourke/AP/PA Photos; 21 Reuters/Ho New; 22–23 Sherron Bridges; 24 (t) Douglas Fretz, (b) Jean Farley/AP/PA Photos; 25 (t) Reuters/Ali Jarekji, (b) Gary Roberts/Rex Features; 26 (t/r, b) www.vipfibers.com, (c) Ashne Lalin; 27 (t) Denis Poroy/AP/PA Photos, (b) Mitsuhiko Imamori/Minden/FLPA; 30 (b) Caters News Agency Ltd/Rex Features; 31 (t) Albanpix Ltd/Rex Features, (b) Phil Yeomans/Rex Features; 32 (t) Photocome/Photocome/PA Photos, (c, b/r) Eric Gay/AP/PA Photos; 33 Michael Steve Bean

Key: t = top, b = bottom, c = center, l = left, r = right, sp = single page, dp = double page

All other photos are from Ripley Entertainment Inc.
Every attempt has been made to acknowledge correctly and contact copyright holders and we apologize in advance for any unintentional errors or omissions, which will be corrected in future editions.